CREE

NATIVE AMERICANS

Big Buddy Books
An Imprint of Abdo Publishing
abdopublishing.com

Katie Lajiness

abdopublishing.com

Published by Abdo Publishing, a division of ABDO, PO Box 398166, Minneapolis, Minnesota 55439.

Printed in the United States of America, North Mankato, Minnesota.
052018
092018

Cover Photo: Marilyn Angel Wynn/Native Stock.
Background Photo: wwing/Getty Images.
Interior Photos: chamey/Getty Images (p. 25); duncan1890/Getty Images (p. 26); fulcrumsf/Getty Images (p. 19); georgewinstonlee/Getty Images (p. 23); Hemis/Alamy Stock Photo (pp. 5, 29); Jérémie LeBlond-Fontaine/Getty Images (p. 21); John Hurd/Getty Images (p.11); Marilyn Angel Wynn/Native Stock (pp. 15, 16, 17); Nikki Carlson/AP Images (p. 27); Scott Gries/Getty Images (p. 30); W. Langdon Kihn/National Geographic Creative (p. 9); William Albert Allard/National Geographic Creative (p. 13).

Coordinating Series Editor: Tamara L. Britton
Graphic Design: Jenny Christensen, Maria Hosley

Library of Congress Control Number: 2017962677

Publisher's Cataloging-in-Publication Data

Name: Lajiness, Katie, author.
Title: Cree / by Katie Lajiness.
Description: Minneapolis, Minnesota : Abdo Publishing, 2019. | Series: Native Americans set 4 | Includes online resources and index.
Identifiers: ISBN 9781532115066 (lib.bdg.) | ISBN 9781532155789 (ebook)
Subjects: LCSH: Cree Indians--Juvenile literature. | Indians of North America--Juvenile literature. | Indigenous peoples--Social life and customs--Juvenile literature. | Cultural anthropology--Juvenile literature.
Classification: DDC 970.00497--dc23

Contents

Amazing People

Hundreds of years ago, North America was mostly wild, open land. Native American tribes lived on the land. Each had its own language and **customs**.

The Cree (KREE) are one Native American tribe. Many know them for their **ceremonies** and handmade crafts. Let's learn more about these Native Americans.

Did You Know?

The Cree call themselves *Iyiniwok,* which means "the people" in their own language.

The Cree language uses its own special characters instead of the English alphabet.

Cree Territory

The people lived in groups called bands. Different bands of Cree lived throughout Canada.

The Woodland Cree lived in the forests of eastern and northern Canada. The Plains Cree moved onto the grasslands of Alberta and Saskatchewan.

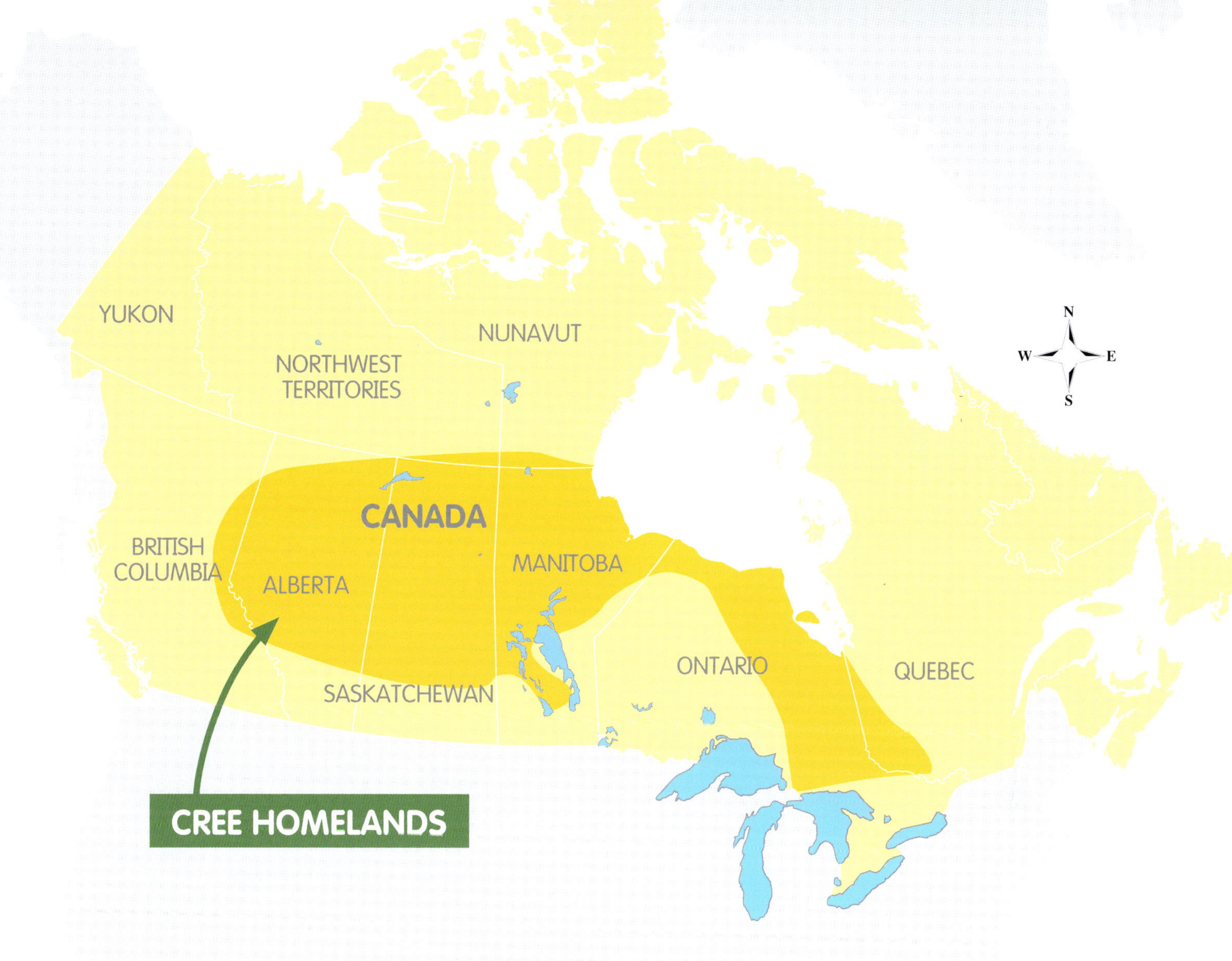
YUKON
NORTHWEST TERRITORIES
NUNAVUT
N
W
E
S
BRITISH COLUMBIA
CANADA
ALBERTA
MANITOBA
SASKATCHEWAN
ONTARIO
QUEBEC
CREE HOMELANDS
UNITED STATES

Home Life

Many small groups of **nomadic** hunters belonged to the tribe. They moved many times a year to follow animal herds. So, their homes were easy to put up and take down.

The Cree lived in teepees covered with buffalo hides, birch bark, logs, or grass.

What They Ate

The Cree hunted buffalo, deer, duck, elk, moose, and rabbit. Fruits, nuts, and vegetables went into the meals. The tribe also ate berries, wild rice, and turnips. And, they hunted seals from boats.

Those in eastern Canada also fished for salmon.

Daily Life

Tribe members made their clothes from animal hides. Everyone had coats, hats, and mittens made from beaver, caribou, or otter skins. Men wore leather moccasins, leggings, and long shirts. Women made their dresses from moose skins.

Did You Know?

The Cree people painted their bodies with tribal patterns.

Cree women decorated clothes with porcupine quills or beads.

Within a Cree tribe, there was a lot of work to do. Men hunted and trapped animals for meat and furs. They also caught fish. Women cooked food and chopped wood. They set up camp and took care of the children.

Did You Know?

The Cree loved to watch horse races.

The Cree used birchbark horns to call for moose. The sound drew the moose close so the Cree could hunt them.

MADE BY HAND

The Cree made many objects by hand. They often used natural supplies. These arts and crafts added beauty to everyday life.

Bear Claw Necklace

The Cree added bear claws to their jewelry. These gave the tribe good luck during a hunt.

Cree Moccasins

The Cree sewed beads onto their moccasins. They often made beautiful flower designs.

Cree Pipe

Cree men smoked pipes during feasts and ceremonies.

SPIRIT LIFE

When a young man became an adult, he went on a **vision** quest. The young man walked alone in the woods and **fasted** for several days. During that time, he had a vision of his guiding spirit. The Cree believed this spirit gave the young man his talents.

Did You Know?

The Cree believe in a spiritual power called *manito* [MAN-ih-too].

The Cree believed spirits came to them in dreams. These spirits protected them during a hunt.

STORYTELLERS

Stories were important to the Cree people. In one story, a man and woman met a spider. The spider helped them reach the ground from a world above. It lowered them down with its web. And it told them not to look down.

When the people did look down, the web stopped. They were left stuck in a tree. Then the couple followed a bear down from the tree. The bear taught them to stay alive. All Cree came from these two people.

The Cree saw the bear as a sign of a great hunt.

Fighting for Land

The Cree have lived in Canada for more than 6,000 years. They first met Europeans in the early 1600s. Over time, the tribe traded furs with the French and British.

By the 1800s, the Cree lived throughout central Canada. Soon, settlers moved onto Cree land. Then, the government forced the tribe to give up their land.

From 1876 to 1906, the Western Woods Cree traded their land to the Canadian government. In return, the Cree received food, shelter, and health care.

In the early 1900s, the government sent Cree children to **boarding schools**. There, they learned English.

From 1920 to 1940, illnesses such as measles and the flu killed many Cree. After **World War II**, the government built schools and health clinics around old trading villages.

In 1828, Fort Union was founded in what is now North Dakota. The Plains Cree and other northern tribes traded there during the 1900s.

Back in Time

1600

Between 15,000 and 30,000 Cree lived in North America.

1781

An illness called smallpox killed about half the Cree people.

1870s

Most of the buffalo died. So, the Cree could not find much to eat.

1880s

Christians spoke to the Plains Cree about Christian beliefs. Many Cree added those new beliefs to the faith they already had.

1950s

The government started building railroad tracks and roads through the Cree's hunting land.

2010

A flood damaged the Rocky Boy Indian **Reservation** in Montana. The government gave money to help the Cree people rebuild their homes.

2017

Dry weather forced the tribe to use less water for everyday life.

The Cree Today

The Cree have a long, rich history. Many remember them for hunting buffalo and telling their **traditional** stories.

Cree roots run deep. Today, the people have held on to those special things that make them Cree. Even though times have changed, many people carry the traditions, stories, and memories of the past into the present.

Did You Know?

Today, there are about 200,000 Cree in the United States.

In Quebec, Cree people continue to trap animals and follow many traditional practices.

"When the last tree is cut, the last river poisoned, and the last fish dead, we will discover that we can't eat money."

— Alanis Obomsawin, Cree

GLOSSARY

boarding school a school at which most of the students live during the school year.

ceremony a formal event on a special occasion.

Christianity (krihs-chee-A-nuh-tee) a religion that follows the teachings of Jesus Christ. Christians are people who practice Christianity.

custom a practice that has been around a long time and is common to a group or a place.

fast to go without eating food.

nomadic of or relating to people that travel from place to place.

reservation (reh-zuhr-VAY-shuhn) a piece of land set aside by the government for Native Americans to live on.

traditional (truh-DIHSH-nuhl) relating to a tradition, which is a belief, a custom, or a story handed down from older people to younger people.

vision something dreamed or imagined.

World War II a war fought in Europe, Asia, and Africa from 1939 to 1945.

INDEX